GERALD F. FISCHBACH AND F

A comprehensive, friendly, and effective course of study for the development of vibrato on violin, viola, cello, and string bass in private or group instruction.

Dear String Student:

Vibrato is the frosting on our tonal cake. It sweetens the flavor of our sound, and makes it more interesting, more colorful, more complex. Vibrato also adds intensity to our sound. As a tool for strengthening our emotional message, it helps us to laugh and to weep, to sing of love, and to shout in anger.

A well-balanced vibrato can actually make playing feel easier, by helping the left hand and arm to stay well aligned and balanced. Vibrato can also play an important supporting role in connecting notes, when you learn to "pour" your vibrato from one note to the next without stopping it.

And not least important, vibrato is a badge of tonal maturity.

Enjoy your journey to mastery. **Viva Vibrato!**

Gerald Fischbach

Robert S. Frost

Instrumentation

Violin   Viola   Cello   String Bass
Piano Accompaniment   Teacher's Manual & Score

ISBN 0-8497-3373-1

KJOS Neil A. Kjos Music Company • San Diego, California

I. VIBRATO READINESS

Vibrato is a balanced, rocking movement. It is much like waving hello, knocking on a door, salting your food, or patting a dog. When you are balanced, the vibrato rocks easily; vibrato "just happens." When you are out of balance, muscles tighten, parts of you squeeze and pinch, and vibrato is difficult.

Before we actually begin vibrato exercises, let's run through a Vibrato Readiness Checklist.

Vibrato Readiness Checklist

☑ **Body.** Does your body swing easily backward and forward, from left to right, and around in small circles? Of course it does! You've been an expert at those motions since long before you learned to play. Do these gentle movements again, and notice how easily you move.

Now place your instrument in playing position. Again, move left to right, back and forward, and in small circles. Are you still moving as easily? If so, good; you have successfully included your instrument into your balanced body system. If not, ask your teacher if you are holding (balancing) your instrument correctly.

☑ **Arm.** Put your left hand in playing position. Does your elbow swing freely? If not, you are tense in the shoulder, and you may have the elbow too high or too low. Move the elbow. Can you now release some left arm tension that perhaps you didn't even know you had? Swing your left elbow again.

Now it's time for our first **Swingercise!**

 **#1: SWINGPLOP**

Photo #1

1. With your instrument in playing position, use your legs and knees to keep it steady and secure. Let your left arm hang by your side. Now swing your left arm in a lazy arc, forward and backward.
2. After a few lazy swings, use a forward *swing* to toss the hand up and over the instrument, then drop the arm so that the fingers *plop* on the fingerboard. Let the fingers "spring" a little on the fingerboard. See *Photo #1*.
3. Do Swingplop three to five times.

Photo #2

☑ **Hand.** In playing position, does your hand balance easily on the end of your forearm? Does it move freely from the wrist? Check the line from fingers through hand and forearm to elbow: there should be no unusual bends or kinks. See *Photo #2*.

Photo #3

☑ **Thumb and Fingers**. No squeezing allowed! Tap your thumb. It should be flexible, touching the cello neck toward the inside edge, not the center, of the thumb pad. See *Photo #3*.

Tap your fingers. They should bounce and float, touching the string on the fleshy pad behind the fingernail, where delicious tone is found, not near the nail, where you may produce a more pinched sound.

Contact should be made with just the thumb and finger pad; if anything else is touching your vibrato will get stuck. Take care not to collapse the hand or pinch the neck like a lobster claw!

Photo #4

 **#2: HAPPYTAPPY**

1. Tap your thumb again. Tap, tap, tap! Now tap your third finger. Tap, taptap, tap! And again the thumb.
2. Now third and fourth together. Then thumb. Now fourth alone. And (guess what?) thumb.
3. Next, middle fingers together, then thumb. Then second alone, and thumb.
4. Now first and second, followed by thumb. And first alone, then thumb.
5. Now mix them up some more, switching regularly between fingers and thumb. See *Photo #4*.

Photo #5

 **#3: SHAKE, RATTLE, AND ROLL**

1. Without your instrument, hold in your left hand a (real or imaginary) matchbox half-filled with rice kernels.
2. Now with your left hand, knock on an imaginary door in front of you. As you shake and rattle, roll your arm around to simulate your playing position. See *Photo #5*.
3. Continue the shake and rattle as you play vibrato on your on your "air" cello.

   Extra tip: it can be fun and instructive to do *Swingercise #3* with both hands, mirroring the actions of the left hand with the right.

☑ With our Vibrato Readiness Checklist in good order, it's time to move on to actual vibrato exercises, and to give birth to a beautiful new **vibrato!**

II. THE BIRTH OF A VIBRATO

A selection of the exercises in this section should be repeated every day, even two or three times through the course of a day, until your vibrato is born, and for a while thereafter. Some will be more useful to you than others; your teacher will help you decide from week to week which combination of exercises is best for you. You will probably be doing these exercises for several weeks to several months. Vibrato comes sooner to some than to others, but everyone gets it eventually.

You should do these exercises during your regular daily practice sessions, of course. Additionally, some of them are good "TV Games"—they can be done while doing other things, such as reading or even watching television! The more often you practice these movements each day, the sooner your vibrato will come.

Photo #6

 **#4: HANDPATS**

1. With your instrument in playing position, place your left thumb on the cello rib near the neck.
2. Now with the side of your left hand, pat the rib. Patpatpat! Let your whole arm follow in motion with the hand. The thumb stays in one place. See *Photo #6*.
3. You can do Handpats with your hand placed at the curve of the cello's shoulder as well. Let the thumb rest comfortably on the rib. Try out both locations.
4. Handpat Rhythms. Pat the following rhythm patterns 10 times each:

Photo #7

 **#5: TOPTAPS**

1. Put your instrument in playing position, and use your legs and knees to hold it steady and secure.
2. With your left thumb pad on the high string edge of the fingerboard in the middle to high register, swing your hand over the fingerboard and tap on the C string edge of the fingerboard.
   - For right now, just to get the "swing" of it, tap at moderate, comfortable speed, in no particular rhythm.
   - Your hand and fingers should be very loose and floppy, with curved, springy fingers. See *Photo #7*.

3. Name rhythms. Tap "Jiminy Cricket! Jiminy Cricket!"

   Tap your teacher's name. Tap *your* name. Tap the names of some of your friends!

   Write the rhythm of your teacher's name here: _____

   Write the rhythm of your name: _____

Photo #8

Photo #9a

Photo #9b

Photo #9c

4. Toptap Rhythms. To the following rhythms, tap the C string edge of the fingerboard as in Step 2. During the rest, swing your hand up and back towards first position, as a kind of "windup" to the next Toptap. Stay above the fingerboard with the fingers. Pivot on the thumb, which stays in place. See *Photo #8*.

Tap the following rhythm patterns 10 times each ($\quarternote$ = 60):

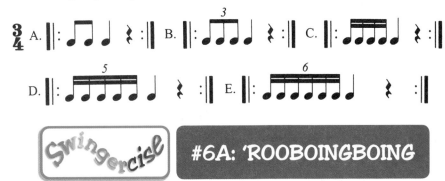

 **#6A: 'ROOBOINGBOING**

1. With your cello in playing position, close your left fingers into a gentle fist.
2. In about fifth position, start bouncing your hand on the fingerboard, like a hopping kangaroo.
3. Now bounce forward, to the higher positions, gradually to near the end of the fingerboard.
4. Next, bounce backward, gradually back to about fifth position.
5. Continue backward, eventually to first position; then turn around, and hop back to about fifth position. See *Photo #9a*.
6. Repeat Steps 2–5 three or four times.

 **#6B: CHICKEN WING**

1. Bring the left fingers together into a point.
2. Place the tip of the fingers into the left shoulder.
3. Raise your left elbow so that it is not quite parallel to the floor.
4. Rock your forearm at the wrist up and down, in a vibrato motion.
5. Do the same with your right arm, together with your left.

 #6D: STRING POLISHING (CONTRACTING WOBBLE)

1. Hold your cello in playing position with your left hand in about fifth position.
2. Sliding up and down the fingerboard, polish a string with one of your middle fingers.
   • Polish most of the string, from first position to near the end of the fingerboard.
   • Slide on the fleshy finger pad.
   • Slide light as a feather.
   • When you change directions, the finger should flex a little, from all joints.
   • Notice that in the lower positions, the thumb is also polishing the neck. See *Photo #9b*.
   • As you move to the upper positions, the thumb comes around from under the neck and glides on the string behind the fingers. As you move back to the lower positions, the thumb tucks back under the neck. See *Photo #9c*.
3. Now gradually make the polishing motion smaller and smaller, and a little faster.
4. Eventually, the finger pad centers on one spot, somewhere around fifth position. The thumb is still polishing.
5. Now anchor the thumb, under the 2nd finger.
6. Repeat steps 2–5 five times.

#7: THE PARADE WAVE

Photo #10

1. With your instrument in playing position, bring your left hand up to about fourth position. Open the hand so that the palm is above the strings facing the fingerboard. Now wave to your cello!
2. Pick up your bow. Play long, slow strokes on the D string. Wave to your cello again. Listen to your pretty vibrato! See *Photo #10*.
3. Play your Parade Wave Vibrato on other strings.
4. Play *Wave Duet* using your Wave Vibrato on Part A, which should be played entirely using open strings. Play Part B using smooth string crossing waves.

1. Wave Duet

Hermann Op. 20, no. 2

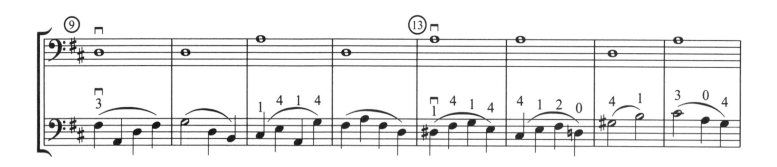

Photo #11

#8: 'TWEENTAPS

1. *'Tweentaps* is just like *Toptaps* (*Swingercise #5*), except it is performed on the finger-board, in a high position, *in between* your D and A strings.
2. Go through the Toptap Rhythms again, 10 times each. (See page 5.)
3. Use your second or third finger.
4. Be sure your wrist and finger joints stay springy and flexible.
5. Do aim for the space in between strings; if you tap on a string instead, you may find your fingers and wrist getting stiff. See *Photo #11*.

#9: HANDSHINE

1. With the palm of your right hand facing you, place the tip of your left thumb in your right palm. Now embrace your left thumb loosely in your right fist.
2. With a handshaking motion of the left hand and arm, use your middle fingers to gently polish the back of your right hand and wrist. See *Photo #12*.
   • Feel the left hand swinging from the bottom of the thumb, way down near the wrist.
   • There should be free movement from all joints of the finger, thumb, and wrist.
3. Gradually narrow the motion so that the second or third finger pad settles into one spot.

Photo #12

Photo #13

#10: STRINGSHINE

Now we will move *Handshine* to the cello. With your thumb in fourth position, polish the D string as in steps 2–3 of *Swingercise #9*. See *Photo #13*.

Let's Rap!

2. Rap Music

1. Play the following "Rap Tune" to *Swingercise #8, 9,* or *10.*

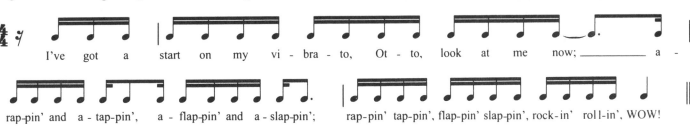

I've got a start on my vi - bra - to, Ot - to, look at me now; _____ a -

rap-pin' and a - tap-pin', a - flap-pin' and a - slap-pin'; rap-pin' tap-pin', flap-pin' slap-pin', rock-in' roll-in', WOW!

2. Make up and tap out your own Rap Tunes!

#11: STICKYTAPS

Stickytaps is just like *'Tweentaps*, with one important difference: magic super glue!

1. Put a drop of this (pretend) magic super glue on your third finger pad.

2. Now start *'Tweentaps*, using the Toptap Rhythms. ♩ = 60. Tap the following rhythm patterns 10 times each:

3. Here's the magic part:

- On the first tapping of each rhythm, the super glue has no effect—tap as usual.
- On the second, the glue works instantly, and you continue the tapping motion with your finger stuck to the fingerboard. Notice how flexible your finger and wrist joints are.
- On the rest before the third tapping, the super glue magically lets go, so that you tap again as usual.
- Continue through the 10 repetitions with the odd-numbered repetitions "unglued," and the even-numbered ones "glued."

Now let's take your "magic super glue" vibrato on a ride to one of the moons of Jupiter!

3. Sunrise on Ganymede
Fischbach-Frost

4. Merry Maiden Waltz
Lehár

You may find that by now you have a functional, if young, vibrato started. Do the next two *Swingercises* if you need just a little more help. They are also useful as an alternative to one or more of the previous *Swingercises*; your teacher will guide you through the best pathway to success for you.

Swingercise #12: THE WAWA

Some electric guitar amplifiers have a "wawa" circuit—a sort of wild electronic vibrato whose speed the player manipulates via a pedal. It works like a car's gas pedal: the more you push it, the faster it goes. The following exercises, which work a little like a wawa pedal pushed to various speeds, are to be played with a metronome, first without, then with the bow.

1. Put your instrument in playing position, use your legs and knees to hold it steady and secure.
2. With your hand in fourth position and the thumb at the crook in the neck, place your 2nd finger on B♭ on the D string. Now do a "Wawa": rock your arm and hand forward and back. The forward-back cycle should feel like one action with a rebound. Do several more in a row, at a tempo that is comfortable for you.

   You and your teacher may find it is better for you to do the Wawa with a backwards action and a forward rebound. Eventually, we don't pay attention to whether the motion starts forward or backward.
3. Wawa with your 3rd finger, B on the D string.

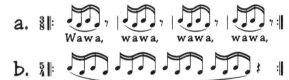

In example (a) the higher notehead represents the vibrato impulse, and the lower notehead is the passive rebound. Thus there are two vibrato impulses per measure, one per 8th-note beat (eight in ex. b).

4. Do the above with your first finger (A on the D string), then your fourth (C on the D string).

Swingercise #13: WEEKLY WAWA

Now we will take our Wawa through a metronome acceleration trip that will lead us to vibrato's doorstep in three weeks!

Week I: Record your progress using the **Metronome Acceleration Checklist** found on the inside back cover. On each day of Week I, play the following exercise and song four times at each of the settings indicated for that day. Note that each day starts and ends two markings faster than the previous day.

5. Waawaa ♪ = 80 – 155 or 80 – 152
Play this finger pattern on all four strings.

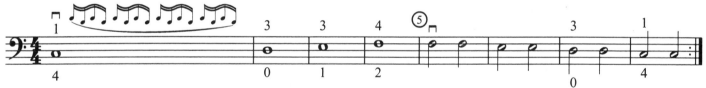

6. Painting a Rainbow ♪ = 80 – 155   Wohlfahrt Op. 38, no. 47
Play this piece using separate bows and also observing the dashed slurs.

Week II: To the following exercise and songs, continue the Week I plan. (See **Metronome Acceleration Checklist** on the inside back cover) Notice that we are continuing with the metronome clicking half as frequently. There are now two complete vibrato cycles per click.

7. Wawawawa ♩ = 70 – 145 or 72 – 132

Play this finger pattern on all four strings.

8. Ring Out the Old (Two-Part Round)

French

The asterisk ✳ indicates the time for the second entrance of the melody.

9. Jacob's Ladder

Spiritual

Play this piece starting down bow (⊓) as well as up bow (∨) for further development of your vibrato.

10. Squid Dreams

Hohmann Bk. 1, no. 49

Play this piece using separate bows and also observing the dashed slurs.

11. Sven's Snowshoes

Norwegian Folk Song

Week III: To the following exercise and songs, continue the weekly plan as before, but advance the   11
speed range only one notch from day to day. Again, see the inside back cover for the **Metronome
Acceleration Checklist.**

12. wwwWOW! ♩ = 135 – 180 or 120 – 180

Play this finger pattern on all four strings.

13. Yorkshire Pudding
English Folk Song

Play this melody using separate bows and also observing the dashed slurs.

14. Moldau Mood (Round)
Bohemian Folk Song

The asterisk ✳ indicates the second entrance of the melody.

15. Sluggo the Singing Snail
Hohmann Bk. I, no. 91

Remember: s n a i l s   s i n g   s l o w l y !

16. Sad Sam's Serious Song
Wohlfahrt Op. 38, no. 41

96CO

III. THE DEVELOPING VIBRATO

The following tunes and exercises are fun to play, and they help your newborn vibrato become mature in several important ways.

17. Go Tell Aunt Rhody
Traditional

This is surely the saddest song ever written in a major key! Use your widest, wobbliest, saddest vibrato!

18. Wauwatosa Wawa
Wohlfahrt Op. 38, no. 34

Play this piece using separate bows and also observing the dashed slurs.

19. Pierre's Stairs ♩ = 100 – 112
French Folk Song

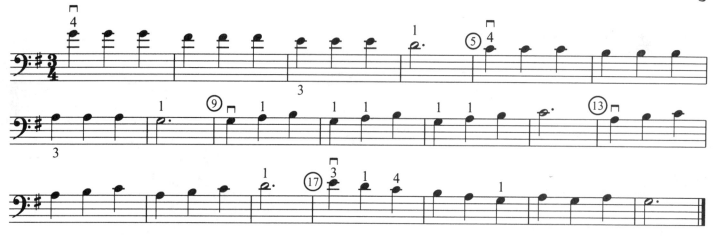

20. Happy New Year (Round) ♩ = 88 - 96
Swiss

21. Dreams of Love ♩ = 88 - 100

Liszt

22. La Folia ♩ = 69 – 72

Corelli

23. Gold and Silver Waltz ♩ = 132 – 144

Lehár

#14: WIGGLEDOWN

A new vibrato that works well in 4th position sometimes is confused at first in the lower positions. "Play" *Sigh!* first without the bow. Notice the change in angle between the wrist and elbow. You may feel more weight at the elbow in the lower positions. Continue to allow the lower arm, elbow, and upper arm to move freely.

24. Sigh!

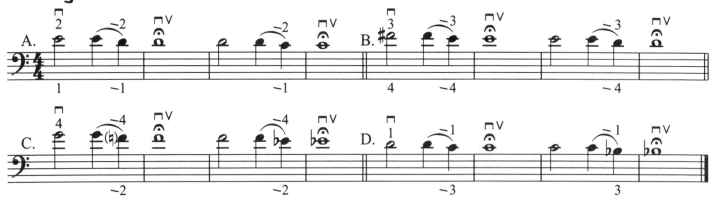

25. Pierrot's Basement Door ♩ = 76   French Folk Song

Slowly play the first phrase of *Pierrot's Basement Door* (A). Create a wide, easy vibrato on each note. In the fermata measures, move your hand back a half step, and play Pierrot again, using the indicated pitches written in versions B, C, D, E.

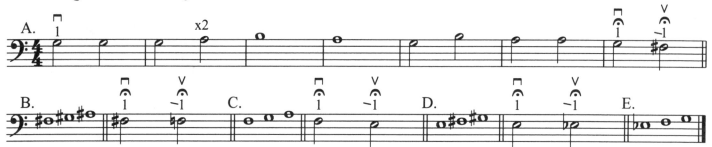

26. Cellar Stairs ♩ = 76   French Folk Song

Play this piece using separate bows and also observing the dashed slurs.

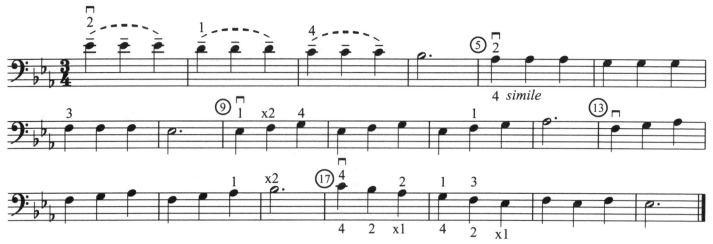

27. Where is John? (Round) ♩ = 92 – 100   Smetana

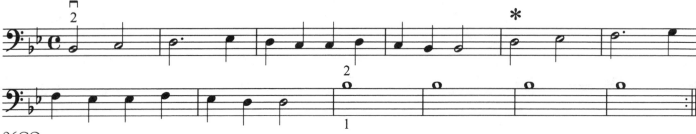

IV. THE MATURING VIBRATO

In this section, your vibrato will develop agility, quick starts, and the ability to move through slurs and shifts.

Swingercise **#15: VIBRATO BURSTS**

These variations on a one-octave scale are intended to give your vibrato a quick start, and to speed up a sluggish vibrato. Each day, choose a different key and different position. In variation A, lift fingers slightly during the rests or in between quarter notes. (♪ ♪ and ♩ mean the same thing here). In Variations B through D, "zap" the vibrato on the accents. ♩ = 60–80 for all variations.

32. Star Bursts
Play Star Bursts using variations A through D from Swingercise #15.

Folk Song

33. Duke Bursts Repetizione ad nauseum ♩ = 88
arr. Fischbach-Frost

34. John Peel ♩ = 116
English Folk Song

35. Vivaldi Goes Ballistic! ♩ = 66
Vivaldi
Accent vigorously with the vibrato and the bow.

36. Wiggwobb Waltz

Fischbach-Frost

Play Wiggwobb Waltz in various octaves, positions, and keys. For every two slurred notes, have just one continuous vibrato.

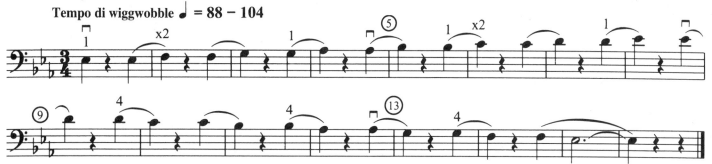

37. Graceful Skaters Waltz ♩ = 104 – 116

Fischbach-Frost

Imagine a graceful skater moving from foot to foot on every downbeat, weight and balance shifting smoothly. With your vibrato, do the same from finger to finger. Pour the vibrato from one finger to the next, so that it doesn't stop between notes.

38. Long, Long, Ago ♩ = 84

Bayley

Keep the vibrato alive through the slurs.

39. All Through the Night ♩ = 96

Welsh Folk Song

40. Shiggle, Shiggle ♩ = 56 – 60

Anderson-Frost

Keep the feeling of vibrato going through the shift. Finger pressure should be as light as possible, especially during the shiggle (shift/wiggle).

FROM: ALL FOR STRINGS - BOOK 3 © 1990 Neil A. Kjos Music Co.

41. Slippery Sal Slides Softly ♪ = 72

Fiorillo

42. Paco's Bell ♪ = 76

Pachelbel

43. Going Home ♩ = 76

Dvořák

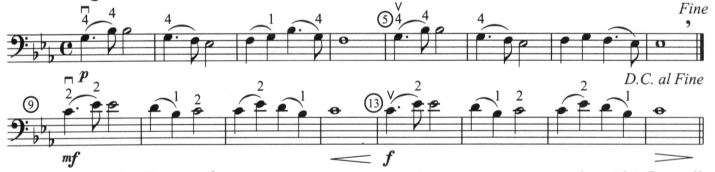

44. To a Wild Rose ♩ = 58

MacDowell

45. Melody ♩ = 76
Rubinstein

46. Londonderry Air ♩ = 56
Irish Folk Song

47. Blessed Spirits ♩ = 76
Gluck

48. Still, Still, Still ♩ = 80
Traditional German

V. THE ARTISTIC VIBRATO

In Part V, you will increase your expressive control, and to learn to think artistically in your use of vibrato.

 **#18: VIBRATO SWELLS**

To various one-octave scales, start measure 1 with almost no vibrato; increase vibrato intensity to maximum at the beginning of measure 2; decrease to measure 3; etc. Use the following meters and note values. Try each variation starting up bow (V) as well as down bow (⊓) for further development of your vibrato and tone. ♩ = 60 for all variations.

49. Chanson Triste ♩ = 88
Tchaikovsky

50. Dolly is Ill ♩ = 66
Tchaikovsky

96CO

To various one-octave scales, manipulate the vibrato width and speed as indicated. Try each variation starting up bow as well as down bow for further development of your vibrato and tone. ♩ = 60 for all variations.

96CO

53. Santa Lucia ♩ = 100   Neapolitan Boat Song

54. Sunset in Vienna ♩ = 120   Frost

55. Silver Threads Among the Gold ♩ = 69   Hanks

56. The Swan ♩ = 58 — Saint-Saëns

57. Austrian National Anthem ♩ = 72 — Haydn

24

58. Piccolo Caprice ♪ = 108 – 144

Paganini

Learn this piece first at a slower tempo, taking care that all eighth notes, especially ones played by the 4th finger, have vibrato. Move the tempo gradually forward to the faster tempo, making sure that vibrato remains continuous.

59. Intermezzo ♩ = 84

Mascagni

96CO